The ABCs of Product Management

Written by Varun Bhartia, Raamin Mostaghimi, and Amit Saraf

Illustrated by Kyle Navaluna

A special thank you to the real Product Managers;

Sean Liu, Justin Charlap, Brittany Cheng, Peter Yang, Monica Garde, Kartik Murthy, Ankit Prasad, Ketan Nayak, Nathan Ie, Carrie Fei, Rutu Samai, Kintan Brahmbhatt, Khalid Ashour

Copyright © 2018 Very Young Professionals Publishing
www.veryyoungprofessionals.com

All rights reserved
ISBN-13:
978-1-7325217-6-6

Product Managers help define what to build and who to build for!

The ABCs of Product Management goes through inside secrets of how Product Managers work.

Your Product Team

PRODUCT MANAGER PANTHER

I've dropped out of Palo Alto Elementary, Harvard Undergrad, and Stanford GSB!

DESIGNER DEER

I got my start illustrating children's books - that makes me a UX expert!

ENGINEER ELEPHANT

Sometimes I write confusing code on purpose just to make myself irreplaceable.

DATA SCIENTIST DOLPHIN

Yes I'm a real scientist, why do you ask? So what if sometimes correlation implies causation?

GROUP PRODUCT MANAGER GERBILS

Performance reviews are only five months away, team!!

VICE PRESIDENT VIPER

Did everybody do the training? Is our product GDPR compliant? What do we make again?

PRODUCT TESTER TURTLE

If there's a bug in the code, I'll definitely find it. And if there's not, I'll make one up.

CUSTOMER CHEETAH

Sometimes I buy things. Mostly for less than it costs to make. Thanks, venture capital!

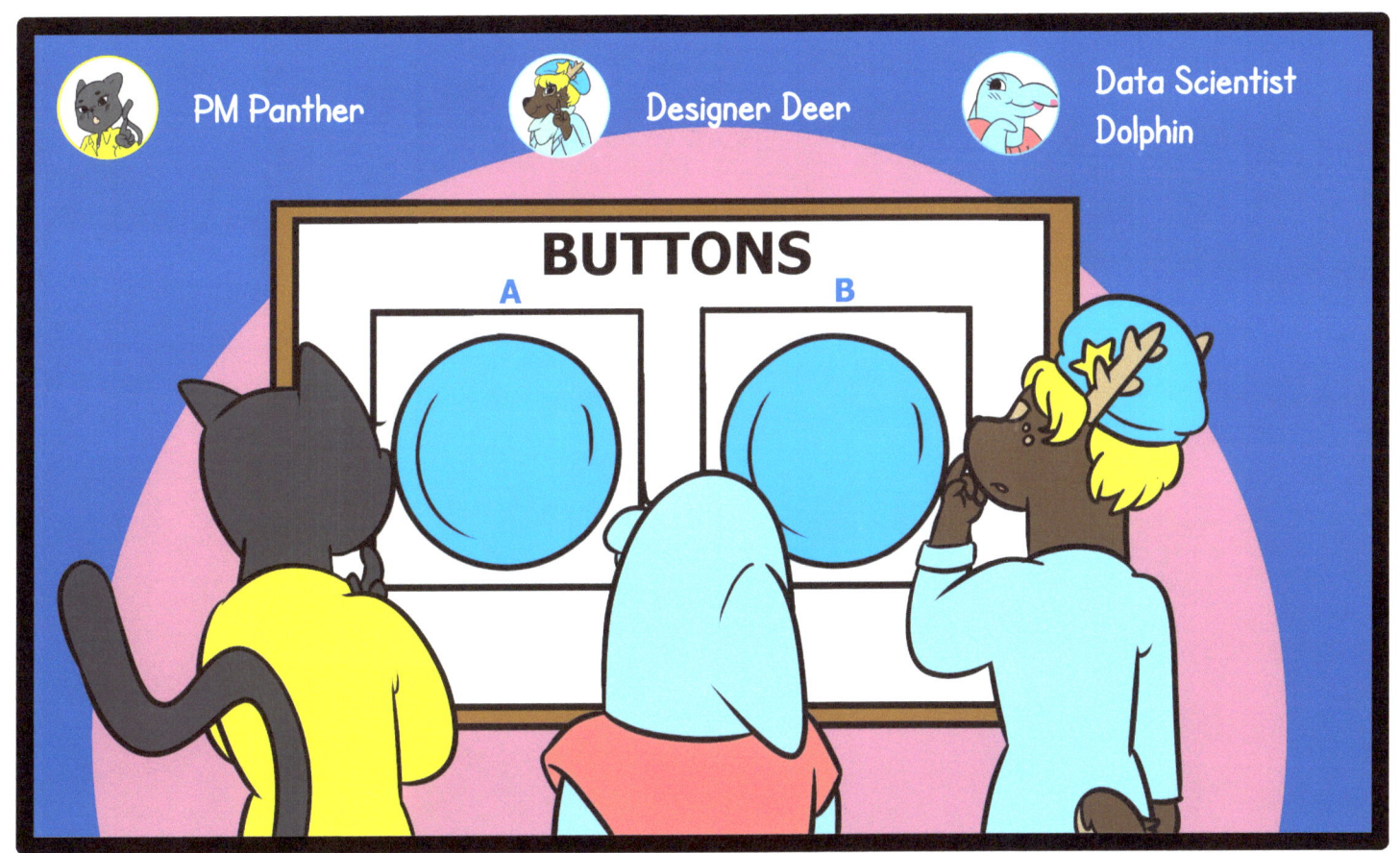

A is for A/B testing

Product Managers will suggest **A/B testing** (testing two different options) when they are sick of arguing with their coworkers about the "right" solution.

B is for **beta**

When Product Managers want to hide the fact that their product isn't ready, and they also want to make their customers feel special, they might say their product is in **beta**.

C is for **customer research**

*Usually, Product Managers conduct **customer research** to justify things they've already decided to build.*

D is for **data-driven**

*Experienced Product Managers don't need lots of numbers to explain their decisions, they just point to whatever makes it seem like someone smart agrees with them and call their decisions "**data-driven**".*

E is for **exec review**

Product Managers have to present their products to their bosses in **exec reviews**. Sometimes, experienced PMs will add easy problems that execs can solve so that they can feel important.

F is for FAIL

FAIL stands for First Attempt In Learning! The best Product Managers learn from failures and come back stronger. Their team is there for them!

G is for **growth**

The best product managers know how to prime their product for **growth**, even if it's not ready and nobody wants it quite yet. Creating exclusivity is one of the best tricks for viral growth.

H is for hustle

*Product Managers always have to seem like they're **hustling** to get everything done. Experienced Product Managers know how to make it seem like they're hustling, even when they know all the tricks to not working too hard.*

I is for **iteration**

Good Product Managers will **iterate** often on their products, so that they keep getting better and better. Great Product Managers will release each iteration right before their performance review so they can maximize credit for themselves.

J is for Jill of all trades

Product Managers have to know a little bit about a lot of different topics, so they end up being **Jills of all trades**. Experienced PMs will admit when they don't know something, while junior PMs will make things up.

K is for Key Performance Indicator (KPI)

*Product Managers create **key performance indicators** to measure how they are doing. Experienced PMs will set achievable goals, so that they can be easily exceeded in order to look impressive.*

L is for listen

*Experienced Product Managers always **listen**, or at least make their team feel like they are listening.*

M is for Minimum Viable Product (MVP)

When a Product Manager wants to release a product quickly, but not listen to a lot of complaints, she can just call whatever she decides to release a **minimum viable product, or MVP.**

N is for **no authority**

Product Managers usually have **no authority**. They have to convince their team about what to do next using only data and logic. Experienced Product Managers know to move quickly to bribery.

O is for **on call**

An experienced Product Manager will ask an engineer to be **on call** when she is afraid her product might break down outside of normal business hours. A junior Product Manager will be on call themselves.

P is for **ping**

When a Product Manager wants to talk to someone (or just message them), but they have to sound business-like, they will often say "**ping**" instead of call or text. It means the exact same thing, and should never be confused with ping pong.

Q is for Quality Assurance (QA)

A *quality assurance*, or **QA** team is incredibly important for the Product Manager, because they catch all the bugs that Engineer Elephant left in the final code. If the QA team misses a bug, the PM can help out by pretending the product is still an MVP.

R is for roadmap

Product Managers always have a plan for what they want to do next, which they call a **roadmap**! Usually the plan is based on gut feel and selectively shared data.

S is for **stand-up meeting**

A **stand-up meeting** is when the whole team tries to explain what they're working on to each other, but nobody really understands what's happening. Weirdly enough, it's okay to sit down during the stand-up.

T is for **timeline**

*Because they have no authority, Product Managers will often make up unreasonable **timelines**, or schedules, to create artificial urgency, and hopefully get the job done!*

U is for **up and to the right**

*Every graph should ALWAYS be **up and to the right**. Number of users, engagement, costs, bugs, crashes - it doesn't matter! An experienced PM will consider changing axes on charts to make them trend up and to the right.*

V is for **vision doc**

When a Product Manager has to pretend to know what to do, she will often consult the bunch of random scribblings she wrote down at four in the morning that she refers to as her "**vision doc**".

W is for **workaround**

When things don't go according to plan, sometimes Product Managers will have to come up with quick solutions that go around the problem - called **workarounds**. These are sometimes left in the final product as a way to cut corners. Experienced Product Managers will know to call these "hacks", so they sound more technical.

X is for X (cross)-functional

*A product needs to work **cross-functionally** with many different groups across the company. Often the most successful way is through bartering and begging.*

Y is for **yoga position**

Product Managers often find themselves pulled in so many directions they end up in a **yoga position**. As much as they like to think they are in the warrior position, they rarely are.

Z is for **zero inbox**

Sometimes, getting closer to the mythical "zero inbox" is the only progress a Product Manager can make on a particularly hard day. "Delete All" is the best way to achieve zero inbox.

Thank you for reading!

www.ingramcontent.com/pod-product-compliance
Lightning Source LLC
LaVergne TN
LVHW071029070426
835507LV00002B/89